Houghton Mifflin Science
DISCOVERYWORKS

HOUGHTON MIFFLIN

Boston • Atlanta • Dallas • Denver • Geneva, Illinois • Palo Alto • Princeton

Authors

William Badders
Elementary Science Teacher
Cleveland Public Schools
Cleveland, OH

Lowell J. Bethel
Professor of Science Education
The University of Texas at Austin
Austin, TX

Victoria Fu
Professor of Child Development
and Early Childhood Education
Virginia Polytechnic Institute and
State University
Blacksburg, VA

Donald Peck
Director (retired)
The Center for Elementary Science
Fairleigh Dickinson University
Madison, NJ

Carolyn Sumners
Director of Astronomy and Physical Sciences
Houston Museum of Natural Science
Houston, TX

Catherine Valentino
Author-in-Residence, Houghton Mifflin
West Kingston, RI

Acknowledgements appear on page H28, which constitutes an extension of this copyright page.

Printed in the U. S. A.

ISBN 0-395-98677-x

5 6 7 8 9 10 RRD 08 07 06 05 04 03 02 01 00

CONTENTS

THINK LIKE A SCIENTIST

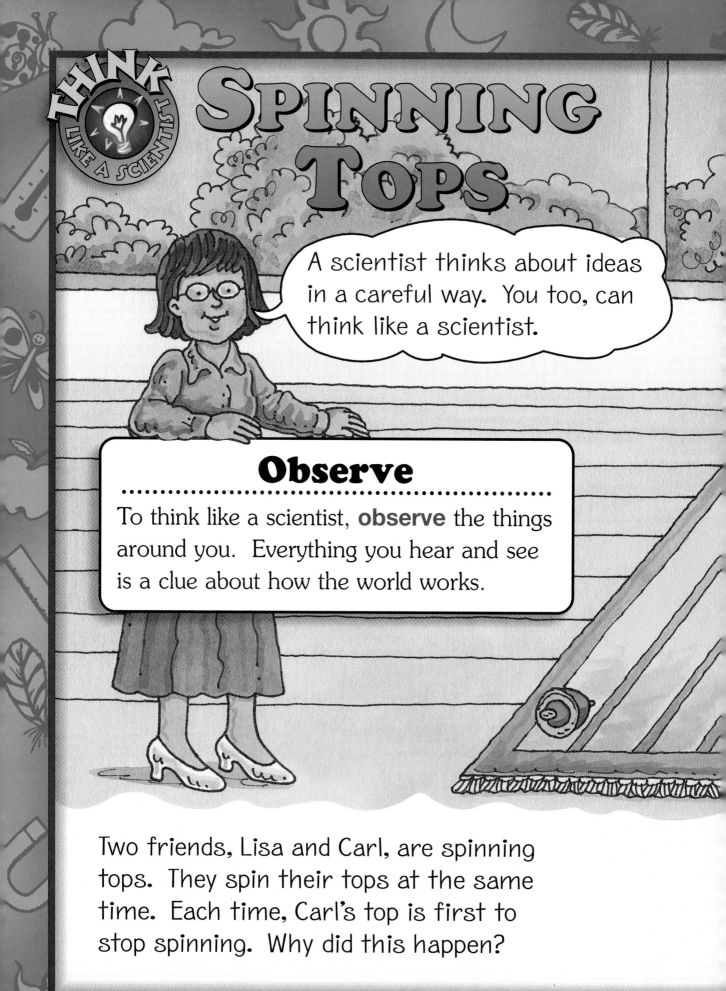

SPINNING TOPS

THINK LIKE A SCIENTIST

A scientist thinks about ideas in a careful way. You too, can think like a scientist.

Observe

To think like a scientist, **observe** the things around you. Everything you hear and see is a clue about how the world works.

Two friends, Lisa and Carl, are spinning tops. They spin their tops at the same time. Each time, Carl's top is first to stop spinning. Why did this happen?

Ask a Question

As you observe, you may see that some things happen over and over. **Ask questions** about such things.

Lisa spins her top on a smooth floor. Carl spins his on a rug. Lisa wonders, does the kind of floor make Carl's top stop first? What do you think?

Make a Hypothesis

Suppose you have an idea about why something happens. You make a **hypothesis**, or a guess based on your idea.

Lisa has an idea about what made Carl's top stop first. She thinks it might be the bumpy rug. How can she find out?

Plan and Do a Test

After you make a hypothesis, **plan** how to **test** it. Then carry out your plan.

Lisa and Carl test the idea. Carl spins his top on the smooth table. Lisa spins her top on the bumpy cement.

Record What Happens

You need to observe your test carefully.
Then **record**, or write down, what happens.

Lisa sees that her top slows down
and stops sooner. She writes down
what happened. What does she write?

Draw Conclusions

Think about reasons why something happened as it did. Then **draw conclusions**.

Lisa thinks about the test.
She decides that bumps cause
a top to stop sooner. You try it!

READING TO LEARN

rosebush

spruce tree

Before You Read

1. **Look** at the pictures.

2. **Read** the words.

3. **Read** the title.

4. **Look** at the **new words**.

Comparing Plants

The same parts of different plants look different. You see fruit on one plant. You see flowers on two plants. The spruce tree doesn't have flowers. It has cones. Both **cones** and flowers make seeds that grow into new plants.

A12 KINDS OF LIVING THINGS

Scientists read to have fun and to learn. You can, too! Just follow these steps.

sunflower

apple tree

The trees grow very tall. The rosebush and sunflower don't grow as tall. The sunflower has big, flat leaves. The spruce tree has thin, pointed leaves. This kind of leaf is called a **needle**. How are other plants different from these?

✔ **Reading Check Draw a picture** of two different plants. Tell how their parts are different.

LESSON 3 RESOURCE   A13

While You Read

1. **Read** the words carefully.

2. **Look** at the pictures again.

3. **Ask** for help if you need it.

After You Read

1. **Tell** what you have learned.

2. **Show** what you have learned.

SAFETY

Wear your goggles when your teacher tells you.

Handle materials carefully.

Never put things into your mouth.

Wash your hands after every activity.

Always tell an adult
if you are hurt.

Be kind to living things.

Clean up spills.

Recycle

Soil

Save resources and
materials to use again.

Throw out materials you
can't use again.

UNIT A

Kinds of Living Things

Theme: Systems

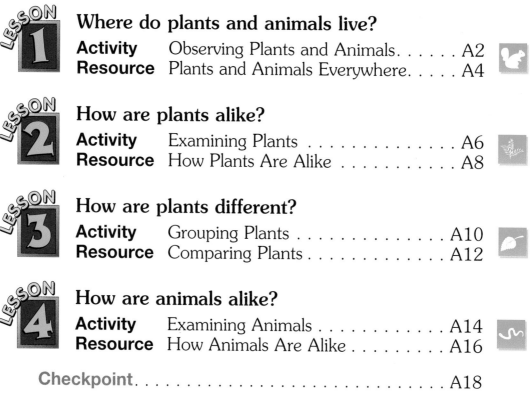

Where do plants and animals live?

Activity
Observing Plants and Animals

What You Need

 crayons

 Science Notebook

1 Take a walk with your class. **Look at** plants and animals.

2 **Draw** the plants you see. **Write** or **tell** about where you see the plants.

3 **Draw** the animals you see. **Write** or **tell** about what the animals are doing.

Think! How are plants and animals different from each other?

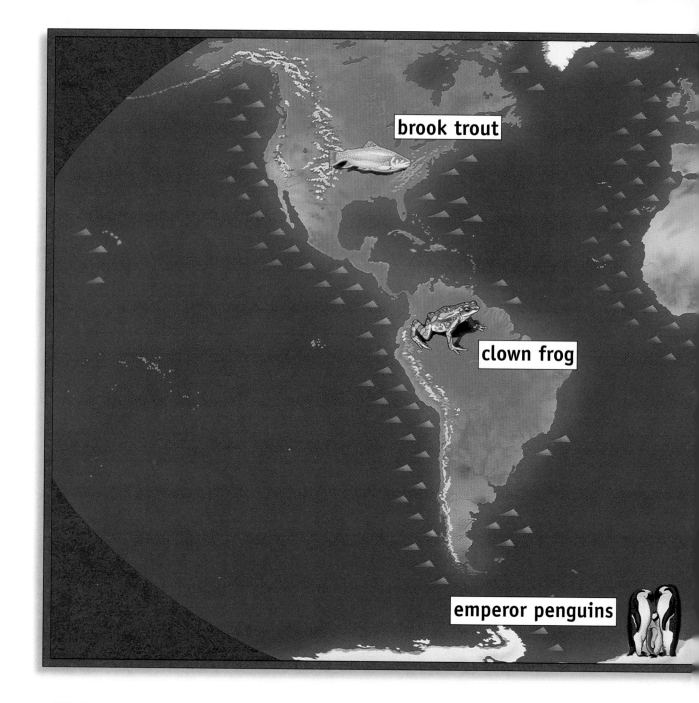

brook trout

clown frog

emperor penguins

Plants and Animals Everywhere

There are many kinds of plants and animals.
They live where they can get what they need to
stay alive. They live on the land, in the water,
and in the air. They live in your home. Plants
and animals live almost everywhere on the earth.

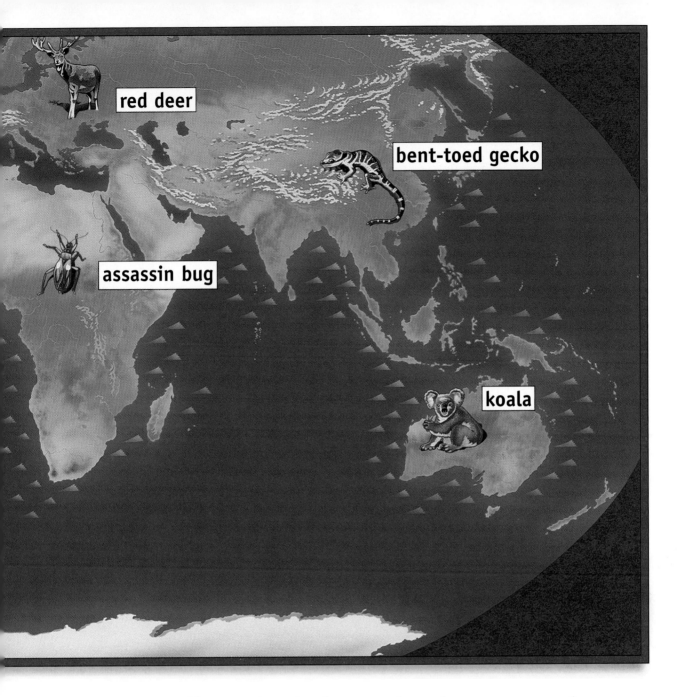

red deer

bent-toed gecko

assassin bug

koala

A different kind of animal is shown on each continent. Each place is different. Some places are hot. Others are cold. Some places are wet. Others are dry. That's why different animals and plants live in each place.

Reading Check Tell about some of the places where different animals live.

LESSON 2

How are plants alike?

Activity
Examining Plants

What You Need

 different live plants 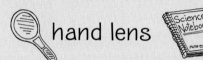 hand lens  Science Notebook

1 **Look at** different plants. Use a hand lens to **look at** the different parts.

2 **Look for** ways that the plants are all the same.

❸ Record your findings.

Think! How are all these plants alike?

Internet Field Trip

Visit **www.eduplace.com** to learn more about plants.

How Plants Are Alike

Plants are living things. Plants need water, light, and air to grow. Plants stay in one place unless moved. Most plants have roots, stems, and leaves. Many have flowers. **Flowers** make seeds that grow into new plants.

Roots grow down in soil. Roots take in water. Most stems grow above ground. **Stems** carry water from the roots to other plant parts. Leaves grow on a stem or up from the roots. **Leaves** use sunlight to make food for the plant.

Reading Check **Write a story** about a plant. Tell what each part does. How is it like other plants?

LESSON 3
How are plants different?

Activity
Grouping Plants

What You Need

 different live plants   hand lens 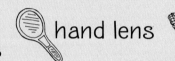 Science Notebook

1 **Look at** the plants and their parts. **Talk about** how each part looks.

❷ Sort the plants into groups.

❸ Make a tally chart to record your groups.

Grouping Plants		
Group	Tally	Total

Think! What makes one plant different from another?

rosebush

spruce tree

Comparing Plants

The same parts of different plants look different. You see fruit on one plant. You see flowers on two plants. The spruce tree doesn't have flowers. It has cones. Both **cones** and flowers make seeds that grow into new plants.

sunflower

apple tree

The trees grow very tall. The rosebush and sunflower don't grow as tall. The sunflower has big, flat leaves. The spruce tree has thin, pointed leaves. This kind of leaf is called a **needle**. How are other plants different from these?

Reading Check Draw a picture of two different plants. Tell how their parts are different.

How are animals alike?

Activity
Examining Animals

What You Need

    different live animals

 Science Notebook

1 Look at different animals.

Some things take in heat from the sun better than others. Things that take in heat better get warmer faster. Dark-colored things usually get warmer than light-colored things. Dry things usually get warmer than wet things.

Reading Check **Tell** why you might want to wear light-colored clothing on a hot day.

How does air move?

Activity
Exploring Wind

What You Need

pinwheel pattern

scissors

tape

pushpin

pencil with an eraser

Science Notebook

1 Cut on the dotted lines of the pinwheel pattern. Stop at the square in the center.

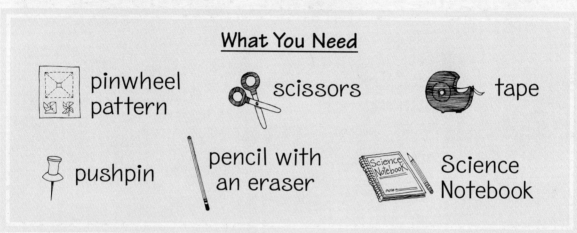

2 Fold the corners with dots in toward the center and tape them in place.

3 Put a pushpin through the center of the pinwheel and into an eraser. Be careful of the point of the pin.

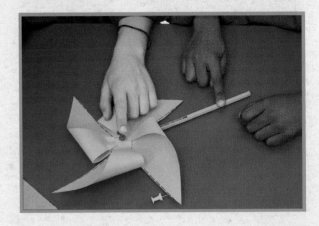

4 **Test** different ways to make your pinwheel turn. **Record** what you try and what happens.

Think! What made the pinwheel turn?

Internet Field Trip

Visit **www.eduplace.com** to learn more about wind.

Blowing in the Wind

Wind is moving air. Sometimes the wind moves fast. Sometimes the wind moves slowly. The wind can move many things.

The wind can make flags wave. Look at the pictures. Why do the flags look different?

In the top picture there is no wind. The air is **calm**. The flag is not waving.

In the middle picture there is a little wind. The flag waves slowly when there's a **breeze**.

In the bottom picture there is a lot of wind. Flags wave quickly in a **strong wind**.

Think of a time when you saw the wind move something. What did it move?

In autumn, wind blows the leaves. It blows the seeds in summer. Wind can blow the hat off your head and keep your kite in the sky. Wind can also move sailboats.

A sailboat will move quickly in a strong wind.
In a breeze a sailboat will move slowly.

The sounds made by the wind can change.
They can be very soft or very loud sounds. What
sounds made by the wind have you heard?

Reading Check Draw pictures to show an
object blowing in a strong wind and then in a breeze.

How does water change?

Activity
Examining Condensation

What You Need

 2 small cans

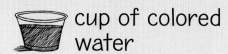 cup of colored water

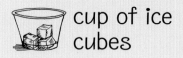 cup of ice cubes

 timer

 Science Notebook

1 Feel the outside of an empty can. **Record** what you see and feel.

2 Put ice cubes into another can. Add some colored water.

3 Use a timer to time 5 minutes. Feel the outside of the can of ice water. **Record** what you see and feel.

Think! How are the outsides of the two cans different?

Find Out More!

Put a wet paper towel in a plastic bag and seal it. What do you think will happen? Check on it in a day. Compare your results with those of your classmates. How did the water change?

Water in the Air

The water we drink is a liquid. Water can also be a solid. **Ice** is solid water. Water can also be a gas. Water as a gas is called **water vapor**.

Look at the pictures. How did the girl make the spot on the window?

There was water vapor in the girl's breath. Her breath was warm. The window was cold. When she breathed on the window, the water vapor changed to liquid water.

Where else do you think you might find water vapor? Where do you find solid water?

High in the sky, water vapor also changes to liquid water. Tiny drops of liquid water form **clouds**. **Fog** is a cloud close to the ground. Fog and clouds are both made of tiny drops of water.

In clouds many tiny drops join to make bigger drops. These bigger drops fall as rain.

fog

hail

dew

    If the cloud is cold enough, the water in it can fall as snow, hail, or sleet.

    Sometimes water vapor near the ground cools. It forms tiny drops of water on objects. The water is called dew, or when frozen, frost.

> ✔ **Reading Check** **Tell** about two ways that water changes.

Word Power

If you need help, turn to the pages shown in blue.

Match the words with a picture. (B18–B19)

breeze   strong wind   calm

1.    **2.**    **3.**

Use these words to fill in the blanks.

clouds   ice   wind   weather

4. The _____ tells about the air outside. (B4–B5)

5. Solid water is called _____. (B24–B25)

6. Tiny drops of liquid water form _____. (B26–B27)

7. Moving air is called _____. (B18–B19)

Solving Science Problems

You are going on a picnic. The weather is sunny. There is a breeze. The temperature is 65°F. Tell what you might wear. Decide what activities you would do. Explain your choices.

People Using Science

Meteorologist

Meteorologists study the weather. They measure and record temperature and precipitation. Looking for patterns helps them predict the weather.

Some meteorologists use computers to help predict the weather. Why is predicting the weather helpful?

 Using a Table

Abby lives in Wisconsin. In December, she recorded the amount of snow that fell each week.

December Snow				
Amount of Snow	**Week 1**	**Week 2**	**Week 3**	**Week 4**
	3 inches	8 inches	6 inches	10 inches

Use the table to answer the questions.

1. In which week did it snow the most?

2. In which week did it snow the least?

3. How much snow fell during Week 1 and during Week 3 in all?

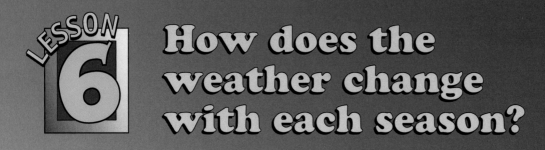

LESSON 6

How does the weather change with each season?

Activity

Going on a Scavenger Hunt

What You Need

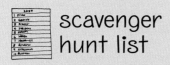 scavenger hunt list paper bag  Science Notebook

1 Go on a scavenger hunt. **Collect** as many items from the list as you can.

2 **Talk about** items that you collected and any items that you could not find.

3 **Make a hypothesis** about how the list might be different in another season.

4 Plan a scavenger hunt list to use during another season. **Record** your list.

Think! How does the season affect what items you can find?

Find Out More!

How does the weather change over seasons? Make a plan to find out. Record the changes you observe.

Looking at Seasons

A **season** is a time of the year. The four
seasons are spring, summer, autumn, and
winter. The pictures show the same place in all
four seasons. Weather changes from season to
season. What changes do you see?

In **spring**, plants bloom and the air gets
warmer. In **summer** the air gets even warmer.
Then in **autumn** it gets cooler. The leaves
may fall off trees. In **winter** the air gets cold.
Trees may be bare. Sometimes it snows.

Reading Check Act out how the weather
changes each season where you live.

LESSON 7
How do people adjust to different seasons?

Activity
Cooling Off and Warming Up

What You Need

 crayons

 Science Notebook

1 **Talk with your group** about ways to cool off on a hot day. **Record** your ideas.

2 **Talk with your group** about ways to warm up on a cold day. **Record** your ideas.

3 Take turns **acting out** your ideas about cooling off and warming up. Have other groups try to **guess** what you are acting out.

Think! How do people cool off and warm up? Explain how you made your decisions.

People and Seasons

What fun it is to play outside! You can have fun in all four seasons.

One picture shows a summer activity. The other picture shows a winter activity. How can you tell what the weather is like in each picture?

People change what they do and wear as the seasons change. In the hot summer, people wear less clothing. Some people swim to cool off. When it is cold in winter, people wear more clothing.

Reading Check **List** things that people do when the weather is hot and when it is cold.

How do animals change when the seasons change?

Activity
Keeping Warm

What You Need

 paper towel

 fiberfill

 ice cube in a sealable plastic bag

 Science Notebook

1 Pretend a paper towel on your arm is an animal's thin summer coat. Put an ice cube on the paper towel for about 1 minute. **Record** how it feels.

2 Pretend some fiberfill is an animal's thick winter coat. Put it between the paper towel and your arm.

3 Hold the ice cube on top of the thick winter coat for about 1 minute. **Record** how it feels. **Compare** your results.

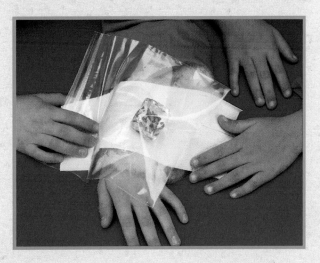

Think! How does a thick winter coat help an animal?

Internet Field Trip

Visit **www.eduplace.com** to learn about how animals and seasons.

Animals and Seasons

Animals also change with the seasons. The first picture shows a weasel in summer. It has brown fur in summer. The weasel lives in the forest. The brown fur helps the weasel hide from other animals.

The second picture shows a weasel in winter. Some weasels live in cold places. Each winter they grow a coat of white fur. This color helps a weasel hide in the snow.

In the spring the weasel sheds its white fur, and a new coat of brown fur grows.

Canada geese

ground squirrels

Animals get ready for winter in other ways. Winter in many places is too cold for some birds. They do not have enough food to eat. These birds migrate. Geese **migrate** by flying to the same warm place every winter. In the spring they return to the place where they started.

American bison

Some animals, like the ground squirrel, **hibernate**. They sleep most of the winter. Their bodies slow down, so they don't need much food.

Other animals grow thick winter coats. The bison's coat keeps it warm in the cold weather.

Reading Check Choose an animal. **Tell** how the animal gets ready for winter.

How do plants change in different seasons?

Activity

Watching Seeds Grow

What You Need

2 parts of egg carton

soil

spray bottle with water

radish seeds

refrigerator

Science Notebook

goggles

1 Put soil in egg cartons. Plant a radish seed in each egg cup.

2 Water all seeds the same amount. Do not overwater.

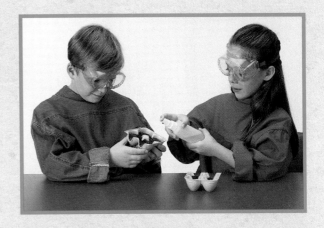

3 Keep one carton in a refrigerator. Keep the other carton in a warm place. Water the seeds every day.

4 **Compare** the two containers of seeds. **Record** what you see.

Think! How does temperature affect how seeds grow?

Plants and Seasons

Plants also change with the seasons. The pictures show an oak tree in each of the four seasons. The large picture is autumn. How can you tell? The leaves have changed color. What seasons are shown in the other pictures?

The top picture is winter. The air is colder. The leaves have fallen from the tree. The next picture is spring. The air has gotten warmer. There are buds on the tree. The bottom picture is summer. There are many green leaves.

Reading Check Write about what the tree will look like next. How do you know what will happen?

Word Power

If you need help, turn to the pages shown in blue.

Match a word with a picture. (B32–B33)

winter   autumn   summer

1.    **2.**   **3.**

Write the letter of the correct word.

4. Birds _____ to warmer places in winter. (B42–B43)

    a. weather   **b.** migrate   **c.** season   **d.** hibernate

5. Ground squirrels _____ for the winter. (B42–B43)

    a. migrate   **b.** season   **c.** hibernate   **d.** clouds

6. _____ from the sun warms the earth. (B14–B15)

    a. Shade   **b.** Heat   **c.** Fog   **d.** Season

7. When water is a gas, it is called _____. (B24–B25)

    a. wind   **b.** shade   **c.** season   **d.** water vapor

8. The _____ of the air tells how hot or cold it is.
(B4–B5)

    a. fog   **b.** clouds   **c.** rain   **d.** temperature

Using Science Ideas

What season is shown? How can you tell?

Writing in Science

Make a chart like the one shown. Fill in what plants look like in each season. Then list what people wear or do in each season. Tell why.

Season	Plants	People
spring		
summer		
autumn		
winter		

Compare and Contrast

The pictures below show how Anita's yard looks in two different seasons. Some things are the same in each season. Some things are different.

Use the pictures to answer the questions.

1. Draw or list the things that are the same in each season.

2. Draw or list things that you see only in the winter season.

3. Tell which things change from season to season.

Measure

Jason got a new weather kit. He likes to use the rain gauge to measure the rainfall. He measured the rain on four different days.

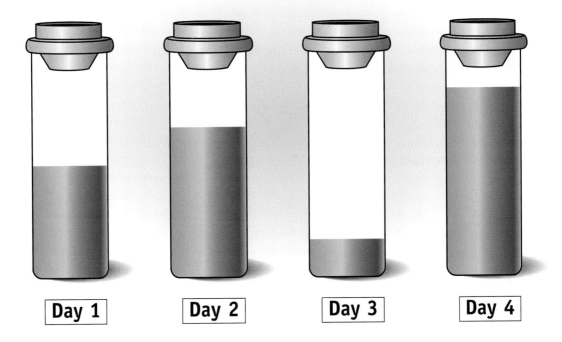

| Day 1 | Day 2 | Day 3 | Day 4 |

1. About how much rain is in each gauge? Record your guess in a chart like the one below.

2. Next, use a centimeter ruler to measure the rainfall in each gauge. Record the measure.

Measuring Rain		
	Guess	**Measure**
Day 1	____ cm	____ cm

Magnets

Themes: Systems; Scale

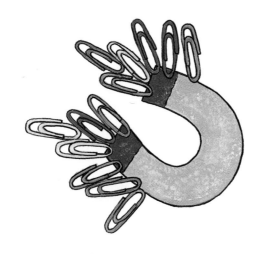

What do magnets attract?

Activity
Exploring Magnetic Attraction

What You Need

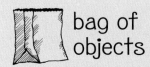 bag of objects 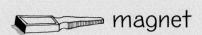 magnet  Science Notebook

1 **Predict** whether a magnet will attract each object. **Record** your predictions.

Exploring Magnetic Attraction		
Object	**Prediction**	**Result**

2 **Test** the objects and record your results. **Sort** the objects.

3 **Compare** your results with your predictions. **Talk about** which results surprised you.

Think! What did you find out about the objects that magnets attract?

Find Out More!

What other things in your classroom are attracted by a magnet? Make a plan to find out. Share your results.

Things Magnets Attract

A magnet is a piece of metal. It can pull some things toward itself and hold them. The magnet **attracts** these things. Look at the picture. Which things might a magnet attract? A **magnet** attracts things made of iron, steel, and nickel.

Magnets do not attract <u>all</u> things. A magnet will not pick up paper or plastic. It will not pick up most soda pop cans. These things are not made of iron, steel, or nickel. What things in the picture will a magnet not attract?

Reading Check **Write** about something that a magnet attracts. What is it made of?

What is magnetic force?

Activity

Discovering Magnetic Force

What You Need

2 pieces of tape

magnet

objects to test

paper clip tied to a piece of yarn

Science Notebook

1 Tape the ends of a piece of yarn to a table.

2 Touch a magnet to the paper clip. Use the magnet to make the paper clip stand up.

3 Slowly pull the magnet up so that it's not touching the paper clip.

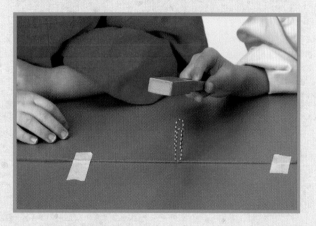

4 **Test** different objects by placing them between the clip and the magnet. **Record** what happens.

Think! Which objects made the clip fall? How are they alike?

Internet Field Trip

Visit **www.eduplace.com** to learn more about magnetic force.

Force of Magnets

Sometimes a magnet can attract things without touching them. A magnet has a force around it. **Magnetic force** attracts things made of some kinds of metal to the magnet. This force can go through the air.

MAGNETS

▲ The magnets attract the paper clips. When the magnets are moved, the trucks also move.

Look at the pictures. How are the children making the trucks move? The trucks have paper clips on them. The magnets and the clips are not touching. The magnetic force from the magnets goes through the air to the paper clips. This makes the trucks move.

Magnetic force goes through air. It also goes through some objects.

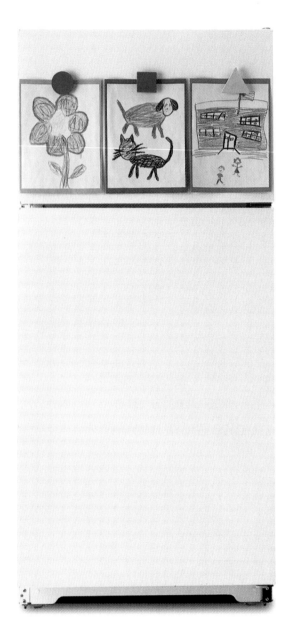

▲ Magnetic force goes through the paper to the refrigerator. All of these magnets can hold up one picture.

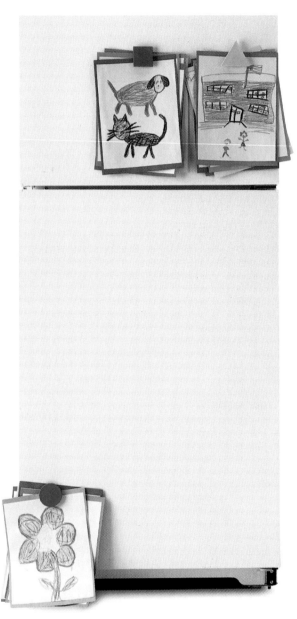

▲ Some magnets are weaker than others. Their force can only go through thin objects.

Some magnets are very strong. Their force can go through thick objects. ▼

Using Math

Use the table to answer the questions.

Magnet	How many it holds
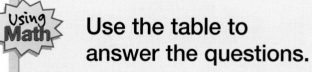	1 picture
■	5 pictures
▲	10 pictures

1. Which magnet can hold 10 pictures?
2. Which magnet is the weakest?
3. How many more pictures can the ▲ hold than the ■ ?

Reading Check **Act out** how it would feel to be a paper clip being pulled by a magnet.

Where are magnets strongest?

Activity
Comparing Parts of a Magnet

What You Need

bar magnet   paper clips   Science Notebook

1. Hold up a bar magnet and make a paper clip chain at one end. Count the paper clips. **Record** the number.

2 Remove the clips. Make a new chain in the middle of the magnet. Count the clips. **Record** the number.

3 Remove the clips and make a chain at the other end of the magnet. Count the clips. **Record** the number.

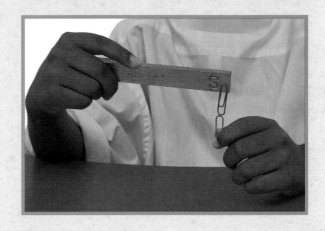

4 Make a bar graph to show the number of clips in each chain. **Compare** the numbers.

Using Math

Clips on the Magnet		
6		
5		
4		
3		
2		
1		
0		
N	Middle	S

Think! What does your bar graph tell you about the strength of different parts of your bar magnet?

Strength of Magnets

Some magnets are stronger than others.
Some strong magnets can pick up a car.

Look at the picture. Which magnet is the
largest? The **bar magnet** is one of the
largest. It is the long, straight silver magnet.

The gray circle or **ring magnet** is one of the smallest magnets. Which magnet do you think can pick up the most paper clips?

You might think a large magnet can pick up more clips than a small magnet. Turn the page to find out which magnet is strongest.

Each magnet picked up some clips. The picture helps you compare the strength of the magnets. A small magnet can be strong. A large magnet can be weak. The bar magnet picked up just six paper clips. The ring magnet picked up many more paper clips.

Find the places on each magnet where you
see the clips. The clips are near the poles.
Magnets are strongest at their **poles**. Poles
are in different places on different magnets.
They might be on the ends or on the sides.

Reading Check **Draw a picture** of two kinds
of magnets. Show where each one is strongest.

Word Power

If you need help, turn to the pages shown in blue.

Match the words with a picture. (C14–C15)

bar magnet   ring magnet

1.   **2.**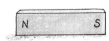

Use these words to fill in the blanks.

attract   magnet   magnetic force

3. _____ goes through the air and some things. (C8–C9)

4. A _____ attracts things made of iron, steel, and nickel. (C4–C5)

5. Some magnets _____ things and hold them. (C4–C5)

Solving Science Problems

Randy and Tara were playing.
Randy said that he could
make his toy bus move
without touching it.
Tell how he could do this.

People Using Science

Crane Operator

A crane operator sometimes uses a special magnet on the crane to lift steel and some other metals. The magnet attracts and holds large pieces of metals.

The electromagnet lifts the metals above large bins. The operator then turns off the magnet and the metal falls into the bin. Why do you think this kind of magnet is useful?

Using Math: Data From a Picture

Look at the picture. Write a number sentence to answer each question. Then solve.

1. How many orange and blue paper clips are there in all?

2. How many more green paper clips are there than yellow paper clips?

4 What do the poles of a magnet do?

Activity

Observing the Poles of Magnets

What You Need

5 bar magnets

Science Notebook

1. Place two magnets end to end and **record** what happens.

2. Turn one of the magnets around and **record** what happens.

3  Place five magnets end to end so that they stick together. **Draw** the line of magnets and label the poles.

Think! How can you line up bar magnets so that they push or pull on each other?

Find Out More!

How are the poles of other magnets like the poles of bar magnets? Ask questions. Make a plan to find answers. Share your results with your classmates.

Attract or Repel?

Bar magnets are on these toys. Look at one magnet. The N shows the north pole. The S shows the south pole.

Look at the train. North poles are next to south poles. **Unlike poles** attract each other.

Look at the boats. North poles are next to north poles. South poles are next to south poles. **Like poles** push away from each other. Like poles **repel** each other. How could you get the boats to connect? Turn some boats so that unlike poles are next to each other.

Look at the photos of the ring magnets. The poles are not marked with N or S. How can you tell if like poles or unlike poles are next to each other? In the first stack, the magnets attract each other. These magnets have unlike poles next to each other.

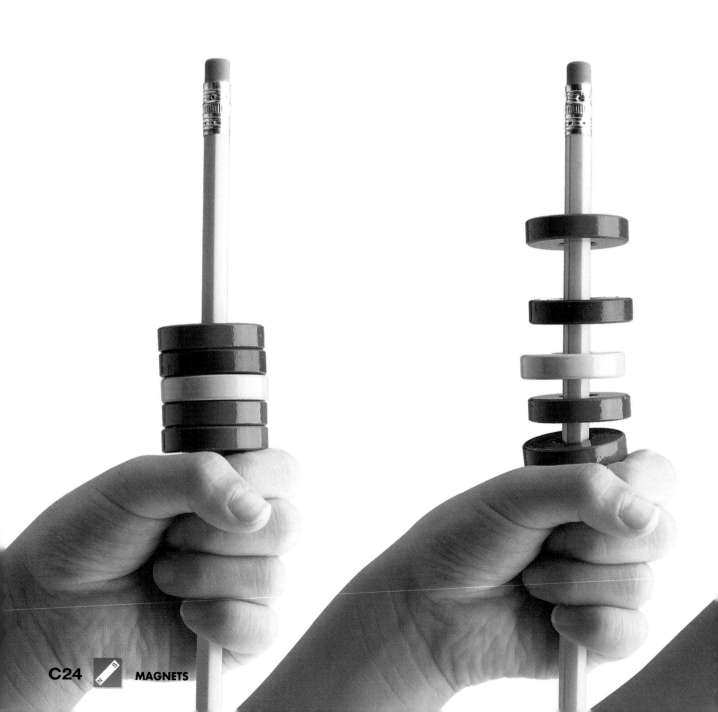

In the second stack, the magnets seem to be floating. These magnets have like poles next to each other. The magnets repel each other.

Look at the two stacks of magnets below. Are the poles next to each other like or unlike?

Reading Check Tell what happens if you put the like poles of two magnets together.

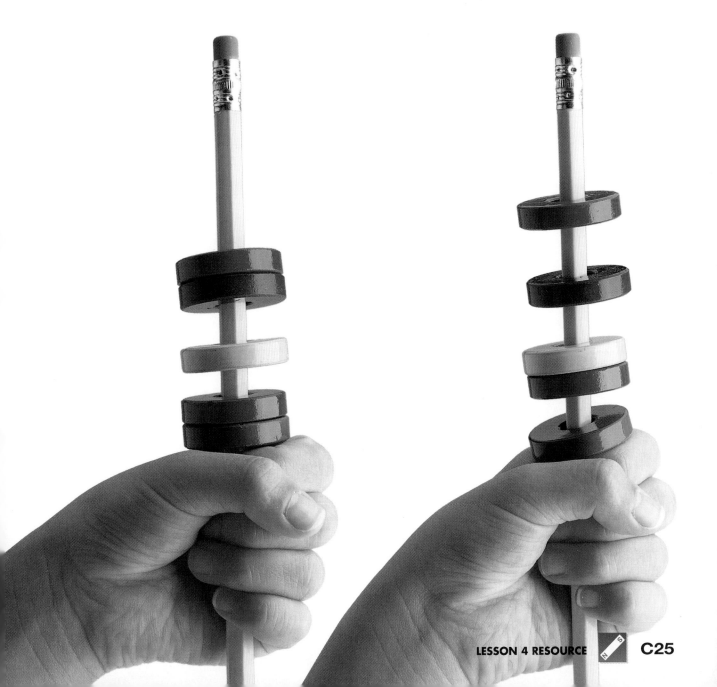

Activity
Making Magnetic Patterns

What You Need

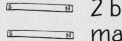 2 bar magnets

 Science Notebook

iron filings in plastic sheet

1 Shake the plastic sheet to spread the iron filings out. **Draw** what you see.

2 Lay two magnets on the sheet end to end. Put two unlike poles next to each other but not touching. **Draw** what you see.

3 Shake the plastic sheet. Then place the magnets so that like poles are next to each other but not touching. **Draw** what you see.

Think! How are your three drawings different? Tell why.

Find Out More!

Use different kinds of magnets. Look for the pattern that the iron filings make around the magnets. Then sort the magnets by the patterns made by the filings.

What's Around a Magnet?

Each magnet can make its own pattern. Look at the patterns. They are made of iron filings.

The patterns show the magnetic field of each magnet. A **magnetic field** is all around a magnet. It's where a magnet's force works.

Look for places where there are the most iron filings. That's where the force is strongest.

Now look for places where there are few iron filings. That's where the force is weakest. What magnets made these patterns? Turn the page to find out.

Think about the picture you just saw. It was made with these magnets.

A sheet of paper was put on top of the magnets. Iron filings were sprinkled on the paper. The filings made patterns. The patterns show the magnetic fields.

Look at the red magnets. Unlike poles are facing each other. Look back at the pattern they made with iron filings. The unlike poles attract each other and the filings. Which magnets have like poles facing each other?

> **Reading Check Draw a picture** to show a pattern made by two magnets and some iron filings.

Activity
Making Magnets

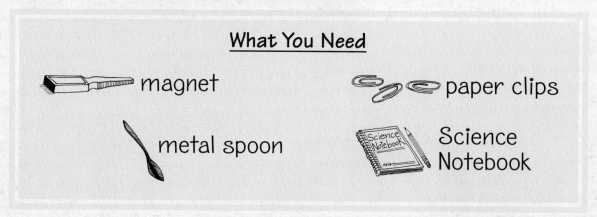

What You Need

magnet   paper clips

metal spoon   Science Notebook

1 Touch a spoon to some paper clips. Lift the spoon and **draw** what you see.

2 Use a magnet to stroke the spoon twenty times in one direction.

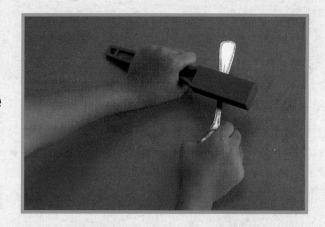

3 Touch the spoon to the paper clips again. Lift the spoon. **Draw** what you see.

Think! Compare your drawings. What happened to the spoon?

Find Out More!

Do you think your spoon magnet is as strong as other magnets? Ask questions. Make a plan to find answers. Share your results.

Making a Magnet

Look at the picture story. The girl wants to fish, too. She makes a magnet. A **temporary magnet** won't last long. The girl strokes a steel key with the boy's magnet. She strokes the key many times in the same direction.

MAGNETS

Think of things that a magnet attracts. You can use any of those things to make a temporary magnet. What can you use? You can use an iron nail or a steel spoon. Why can't you use a plastic jar to make a magnet?

Reading Check **Write** directions to tell someone how to make and use a temporary magnet.

How are a compass and a magnet alike?

Activity

Using a Magnet as a Compass

What You Need

pan of water

bar magnet

plate

magnetic compass

Science Notebook

1 Float a plate in a pan of water.

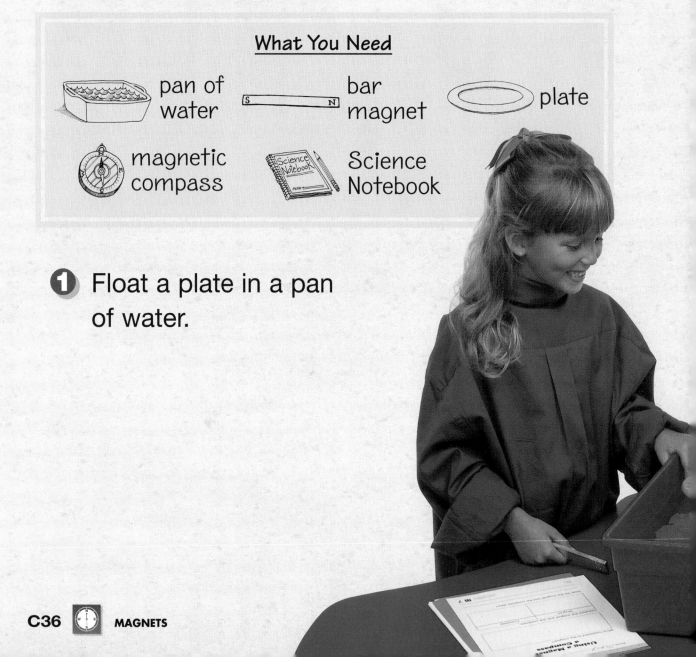

② Put a bar magnet in the center of the plate. **Record** what happens.

③ **Compare** the poles of the magnet with the needle on a compass. **Record** what you see.

Think! How are the poles of the magnet and the compass needle alike?

Internet Field Trip

Visit **www.eduplace.com** to find out more about the earth's magnetic field.

Finding Your Way

The earth is like a bar magnet. It has a north pole. It also has a south pole.

A compass needle is a bar magnet. It has a north-seeking pole. This pole points to the place where the earth's north pole is.

The people in these photos are using compasses. A **compass** is a tool. It is used to show direction. The hikers turn the compass until the needle points to the N. This tells them which way is north.

Reading Check **Tell** a story about using a bar magnet to find your way home.

Word Power

If you need help, turn to the pages shown in blue.

Match the words with a picture. (C14, C34, C39)

bar magnet   compass   temporary magnet

1.   **2.**   **3.**

Use these words to fill in the blanks.

4. A magnet is strongest at its _____. (C16–C17)

   a. south   **b.** attract   **c.** poles   **d.** compass

5. When the poles of two magnets pull toward each other, they are _____ poles. (C22–C23)

   a. like   **b.** unlike   **c.** south   **d.** magnetic

6. The north poles of two magnets push away, or _____ each other. (C22–C23)

   a. repel   **b.** attract   **c.** poles   **d.** bar magnet

7. When the poles of two magnets push away from each other, they are _____ poles. (C22–C23)

   a. north   **b.** like   **c.** unlike   **d.** magnets

8. The area around a magnet where the force is felt is the _____. (C28–C29)

   a. repel   **b.** attract   **c.** poles   **d.** magnetic field

Using Science Ideas

a. Which things shown will a magnet attract? List or draw them.

b. Which things shown will a magnet not attract? List or draw them.

c. Explain how you decided which things a magnet would attract.

Writing in Science

What things do you think a magnet will attract through? Talk about the problem you are trying to solve and some of your solutions. Explain how you would test your ideas. Record your results, and share them with your classmates.

Using READING SKILLS

Predicting Outcomes

Look at each row of magnets. Predict what will happen if you push the magnet on the right side in each row toward the other magnets.

Write or draw your predictions. Use magnets to test your predictions. Then draw pictures to show what happened.

1. S N | S N S N

2. S N N S S N

3. S N | S N N S

4. S N N S N S

Tell how your predictions matched your results.

Making a Table

Susana and Abdul were helping in the school store. Someone dropped a box of paper clips. Susana and Abdul used these magnets to pick up the paper clips.

Make a table like the one below. Use the picture to complete the table.

Picking Up Paper Clips	
Type of magnet	**Number of paper clips**

Use the table to answer the questions.

1. How many paper clips did the three magnets attract altogether?

2. Which magnet would you use to pick up a box of paper clips? Tell why.

UNIT D

Earth's Land and Water

Themes: Systems; Models

What kinds of soil cover the earth's land?

Activity

Examining Kinds of Soil

What You Need

goggles   topsoil   clay soil

sandy soil   hand lens   Science Notebook

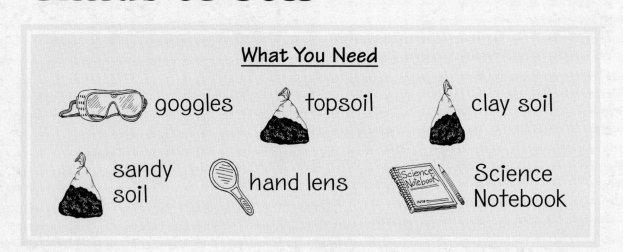

1 **Look at** and touch three kinds of soil.

❷ Look at each kind of soil with a hand lens.

❸ Record what you see.

Think! How are these kinds of soil alike, and how are they different?

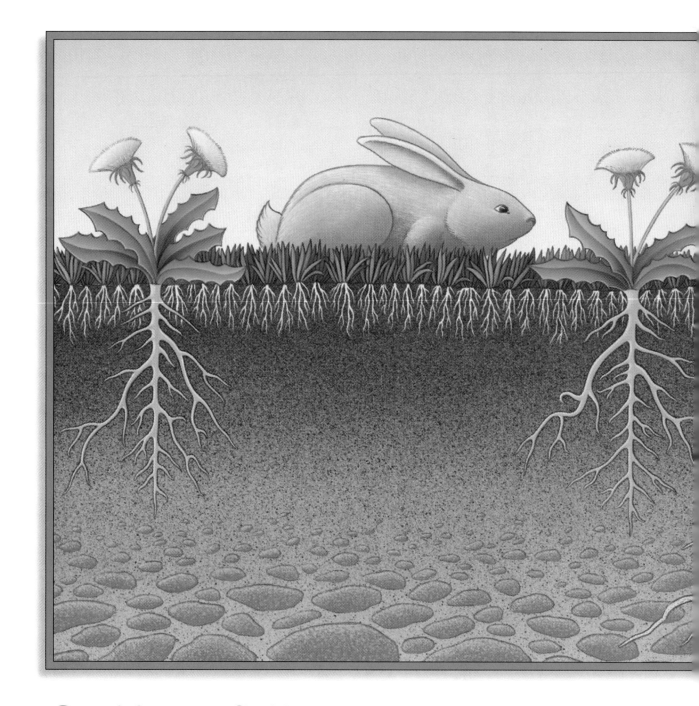

Looking at Soil

Soil covers much of the earth's land. Look at
the layers of soil in the picture. You see grass,
a tree, and flowers growing in the soil. You see
the top layer of soil when you look at the
ground. You don't see the layers under it.

In some places, the top layer of soil is dark
and loose. This is called **topsoil**. Plants grow
well in topsoil. Sometimes **clay soil** is under
topsoil. Big rocks are under the clay soil. Every
place on the earth has rock below it.

Reading Check **Write** about the kinds of soil
that cover the earth. What grows in soil?

What kinds of things does soil contain?

Activity
Analyzing Soil

What You Need

 goggles

 cup of soil

hand lens

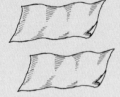 2 large sheets of paper

 Science Notebook

1 Spread out soil on a sheet of paper. Use a hand lens to **look at** the soil.

2 Place things you find in the soil on another sheet of paper.

3 **Group** things that are alike. **Draw** each group.

Using
Math

Think! What kinds of things did you find in the soil?

Looking Closer at Soil

Soil is made of many things. The things in the picture can become part of soil. The logs and the leaves in the picture are **once-living things**. They are not living now. When they were living, they were part of a tree.

A tree is a living thing. **Living things** need air, water, and food to stay alive.

A rock is a nonliving thing. **Nonliving things** do not need air, water, and food. What kinds of things might you find under the log? Turn the page to find out.

The log has been rolled away. What living things do you see? You see plants and tiny animals that live in soil. The hand lenses make them look a lot bigger than they are.

What nonliving things do you see? You see pieces of rock.

Look through the hand lenses again. What once-living things do you see? You see pieces of dry leaves and twigs. These things were once part of a tree. They no longer need air, water, and food.

> **Reading Check Draw a picture** of some things you might find in soil.

What happens to soil when water is added?

Activity

Examining Soil and Water

What You Need

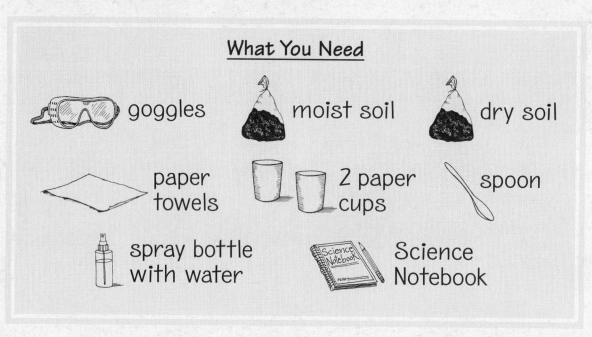

goggles

moist soil

dry soil

paper towels

2 paper cups

spoon

spray bottle with water

Science Notebook

1. Place paper towels under two paper cups. Fill half of cup 1 with moist soil. Fill half of cup 2 with dry soil.

2 Spray each cup 20 times with water. Count to 10.

Using Math

3 Repeat step 2.

4 **Record** what happens.

Think! What happened to the water in each cup? Why did this happen?

Find Out More!

Make a list of questions about plants and what they need to live. Then make a plan to find answers. Use the plan. Tell about what you find.

Water in Soil

Soil is made of tiny rocks and once-living
things. There are many little air spaces in soil.
When it rains, water soaks into these spaces.
If there is more water than the spaces in the
soil can hold, puddles may form.

Over time, some water from the puddles goes into the air. Water from the puddles may also slowly soak into the soil. The water in the soil is used by living things. What living things use water in the soil?

> **Reading Check Tell** what happens to soil after it rains. Why do puddles form?

LESSON 4

How does water move?

Activity

Observing How Water Flows

What You Need

goggles

wet sand

pan

button

measuring cup of water

Science Notebook

1 Use wet sand to make a small hill in a pan.

2 Put a button in a place where you **predict** water will flow.

3 **Measure** one cup of water. Slowly pour the water from the measuring cup onto the top of the hill.

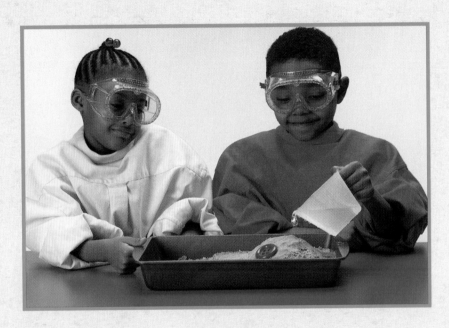

4 **Watch** where the water flows. **Record** what you see.

Think! Where did the water flow?

Internet Field Trip

Visit **www.eduplace.com** to learn about the ways we use water.

Moving Water

Water flows downhill. Sometimes it goes fast. Sometimes it goes slowly.

The first picture shows water moving downhill in a **river**. The water goes fast. When the water reaches the bottom, it goes slowly.

EARTH'S LAND AND WATER

Moving water is very strong. It can cut a
path in the ground. The middle picture shows
moving water in a small river called a **stream**.

Water moves in an **ocean**, too. You can see
ocean waves moving in the last picture.

> **Reading Check Act out** how water moves.
> Where is moving water found?

Where does water gather?

Activity
Observing How Water Gathers

What You Need

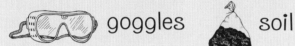 goggles soil plastic dishpan

 3 measuring cups of water Science Notebook

1 Cover the bottom of a dishpan with soil. Push down the soil in the middle.

2 Slowly pour 3 cups of water into the dishpan. **Watch** where the water flows.

3 **Record** what you see.

Think! What happened to the water?

Puddles and Lakes

Water that doesn't soak into the ground
forms a puddle. It can dry up in the sunshine.

Water from springs and rivers can form a
lake. A **lake** has a lot of water in it. Most
lakes do not dry up in the sunshine.

Look at the picture. Where is the river water flowing? It is flowing downhill into a lake.

Lakes need to be kept clean so that the water is safe to use. Then we can have fun there. How might you help keep a lake clean?

Reading Check Draw a picture that shows places where you have seen water gather.

CHECKPOINT

Word Power

If you need help, turn to the pages shown in blue.

Match a word with a picture. (D18–D19, D22–D23)

stream   river   lake

1.
2.
3.

Use these words to fill in the blanks.

living   clay soil   once-living

4. A _____ thing needs air, water, and food to stay alive. (D8–D9)

5. Soil that is under topsoil is called _____. (D4–D5)

6. Fallen leaves are _____ things. (D8–D9)

Solving Science Problems

Look at the picture. Explain what the problem is. Then tell how you could help to solve the problem.

People Using Science

Ecologist

Ecologists study living things and the places where they live. Ecologists might study life underwater, in a rain forest, or in the air. They might study plants to find out where the plants live.

How can studying plants help an ecologist know where different kinds of bugs live?

Make a Tally Chart

Make a tally chart like the one below. Then use the pictures to complete the chart.

Kinds of Things		
Thing	Tally	Total
Living		
Nonliving		
Once-living		

How can rocks be grouped?

Activity
Looking at Rocks

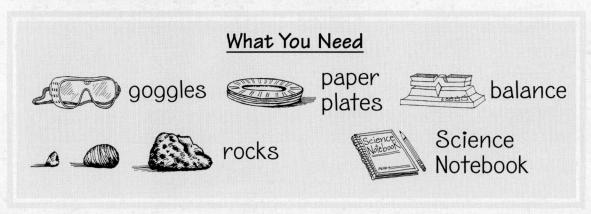

What You Need

goggles   paper plates   balance

rocks   Science Notebook

1 Spread out rocks on a table.
Look at and feel each rock.

2 **Measure** the mass
Using Math of each rock on a
balance.

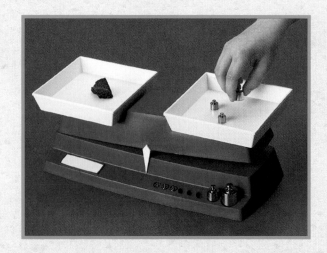

❸ Decide how to **group** the rocks.
Put each group on a paper plate.
Draw each group.

**Think! How did you group
the rocks?**

Internet Field Trip

Visit **www.eduplace.com** to learn
more about rocks and minerals.

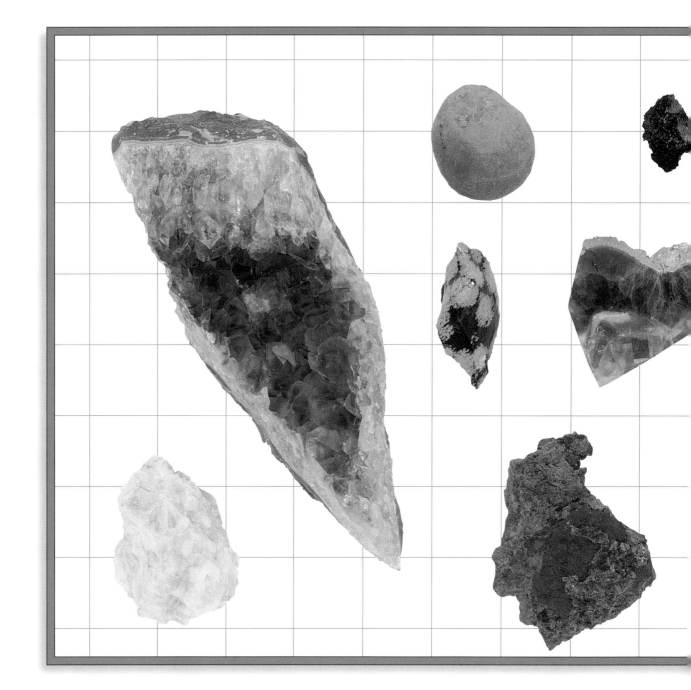

Grouping Rocks

Rocks come in many colors, shapes, and sizes. Look at the rocks in the picture. What color groups could you make? How would you group the rocks by shape? Which rocks would you group together by size?

Rocks can be grouped by the way they feel. Some rocks are smooth. Other rocks are not smooth. They are rough.

The white rock in the picture is rough. Which rocks are smooth?

Reading Check Make a group of rocks from the picture. **Write** about how the rocks are alike.

How can the hardness of rocks be compared?

Activity

Testing the Hardness of Rocks

What You Need

 goggles

 rocks

 tile

 Science Notebook

1 Spread rocks on a table.

2 Squeeze each rock in your hand. **Record** how each rock feels.

3 Use your fingernail to scratch each rock. **Record** what you **observe**.

4 Then scratch a tile with each rock. **Record** what you **observe**.

Testing Hardness of Rocks			

Rock 1			

5 **Compare** the rocks.

Think! Which rocks were the hardest? Tell how you know.

The Hardness of Rocks

Some rocks are harder than others. You can't tell how hard a rock is by looking at it. You need to know more about the rock.

A hard rock can **scratch**, or make a mark on, a softer rock. Soft rocks can't scratch harder rocks.

The artist in the large picture is carving turquoise. It is a hard rock.

The top picture shows sandpaper. The tiny rocks on sandpaper are harder than turquoise.

The bottom picture shows table salt. This salt is softer than the turquoise.

Rocks are used for many things. Hard rocks and soft rocks have different uses.

◄ Graphite is not very hard. It is used in pencils.

Diamonds are the hardest rocks. They are used in jewelry. ▶

◄ Bauxite contains aluminum. Aluminum is used to make foil and baking pans.

Talc is the softest rock. It is used to make powder. ▶

Using Math Look at the table. The highest numbers show the hardest rocks.

Hardness of Rocks				
	Bauxite	**Diamond**	**Graphite**	**Talc**
Hardness	3	10	2	1

Use the table to answer the questions.

1. Which rock is harder than bauxite?

2. Can graphite scratch bauxite? Tell how you know.

3. Put the rocks in order from <u>softest</u> to <u>hardest</u>.

✔ **Reading Check Write** about the different ways the hardness of rocks can be compared.

How large are rocks?

Activity
Examining Sizes of Rocks

What You Need

goggles

rocks

sand

hand lens

Science Notebook

1. Spread rocks and sand on a table.

2. **Look at** each rock with a hand lens. **Draw** what you see.

3 **Look** at the sand with a hand lens. **Draw** what you see.

Think! How are the rocks and the sand alike, and how are they different?

Find Out More!

How many pieces of rock are in a pinch of sand? Make a plan to find the answer. What tools will you need? Compare your findings with those of other groups.

Looking at Size

Rocks come in many sizes. Very big rocks
are called **boulders**.

The picture shows rocks of different sizes.
The very big rock in the front is a boulder. It is
the biggest rock in the picture.

After a long time, moving water wears
away rocks. The water makes the rocks smaller.
What might you find on the bottom of the
river? You might find small rocks and sand.
Sand is made up of tiny pieces of rock.

Reading Check Tell a story about rocks in a
river. Use the words <u>big</u>, <u>small</u>, <u>tiny</u>, and <u>boulder</u>.

How does recycling help the earth?

Activity
Making Compost

What You Need

goggles   soil   2 small milk cartons

spoon   plastic cap   banana peel

spray bottle with water   Science Notebook

1 Fill two cartons with soil.

2 Bury a piece of banana peel in carton 1 and a cap in carton 2.

3 Spray each carton 10 times and then close each carton. Put both cartons in a warm place.

Using Math

4 Repeat step 3 each day for four weeks.

5 Uncover the objects once a week and **record** what you see.

Think! How did the objects change?

Find Out More!

CD-ROM

Composting is a way of recycling. Listen to **Science Blaster Jr.** to hear more ways to recycle.

Using Soil, Rocks, and Water

Recycling means using things again. This woman is making compost. **Compost** is something made by recycling once-living things. Look at the large photo. The woman is adding fruit and vegetable scraps to the pile.

Look at the small photos. The woman mixes leaves and grass clippings with the scraps. Then she stirs the pile. In time these things will break down to become compost.

The woman adds the compost to the soil. Soil is used to help plants grow.

There are many ways to recycle. Even rocks can be recycled. Look at the pictures.

▲ Boulders were found at a building site. A wall was built with these huge rocks.

▲ An old road was crushed to make gravel. These little rocks are under the new road.

Many cities recycle water. Dirty water is sent
to a water-treatment place. After the water has
been cleaned, it is used to water grass.

✔ **Reading Check Tell** how recycling food scraps,
rocks, and water can help the earth.

Word Power

If you need help, turn to the pages shown in blue.

Match the words with a picture. (D8–D9, D38–D39)

boulder   sand   living thing

1.

2.

3.

Write the letter of the correct word.

4. When you use things again, you _____. (D42–D43)

   a. stream   **b.** rock   **c.** scratch   **d.** recycle

5. Water in an _____ moves in waves. (D18–D19)

   a. puddle   **b.** ocean   **c.** sand   **d.** downhill

6. Hard rocks can _____ softer rocks. (D32–D33)

   a. clay   **b.** topsoil   **c.** scratch   **d.** compost

7. The top layer of soil is called _____. (D4–D5)

   a. topsoil   **b.** clay   **c.** sand   **d.** rock

8. You can recycle fruit and vegetable scraps into _____. (D42–D43)

   a. rock   **b.** clay   **c.** scratch   **d.** compost

Using Science Ideas

Look at the picture. List the living things you see. Next, list the once-living things you see. Then list the nonliving things you see.

 ## Writing in Science

A space explorer has found a rock on the moon. You are a newspaper reporter. You need to learn about the moon rock. Make a list of questions to ask about the moon rock.

Reading Skills

Cause and Effect

When the rain stopped, Todd went outside. He wanted to see how the rain changed the soil and rocks. Look at the picture. Make a list of the changes Todd found.

Using Math **Guess and Check**

About how many paper clips long is each rock?
Guess. Then use paper clips to measure.

1.

Guess   **Measure**

about _____ clips   about _____ clips

2.

Guess   **Measure**

about _____ clips   about _____ clips

3.

Guess   **Measure**

about _____ clips   about _____ clips

UNIT E

Keeping Fit and Healthy

Themes: Systems; Constancy and Change

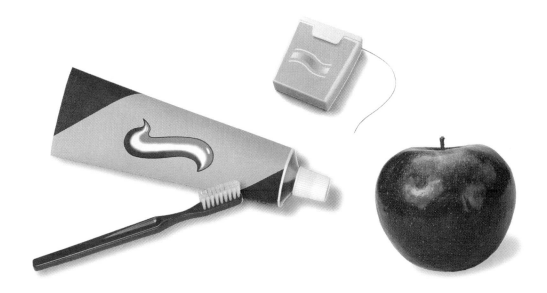

What kinds of food does your body need?

Activity

Grouping Foods

What You Need

 empty food containers

 6 grocery bags with labels

 Science Notebook

1 Bring in empty food containers from home.

2 Sort the containers into food groups.

Using Math

3 Draw a picture of the food in each group. Name each food.

4 Think of other foods to add to these groups. **Tell** why you think they belong.

Think! What kinds of foods should you eat the most? Tell how you decided.

Find Out More!

CD-ROM

Use **Science Blaster Jr.** Go to the Engineering Room to sort out food groups. Collect fruits, vegetables, snacks, and more.

The Food Pyramid

The picture shows a **food pyramid**. It tells about the foods you need each day to stay healthy. The food pyramid tells how many servings of different types of food your body needs.

A roll is one **serving** of bread. An apple is one serving of fruit. You need more servings of some foods than others.

You should eat three to five servings of vegetables each day. What foods do you need two to four servings of each day?

There are six food groups in the food
pyramid. A **food group** has like kinds of food.
Milk, yogurt, and cheese are one food group.
This group has things that are made with milk.
What other foods belong to this group?

Meat, Poultry, Fish, Dry Beans, Eggs, and Nuts
2 - 3 servings

Fruits
2 - 4 servings

Bread, Cereal, Rice, and Pasta
6 - 11 servings

The box at the bottom of the pyramid is the largest. Your body needs the most servings from this food group. The smallest box is at the top of the pyramid. Your body needs the fewest servings from this food group.

Reading Check List the six food groups. Name some of your favorite foods in each group.

2

What is a balanced meal?

Activity

Fishing for a Balanced Meal

What You Need

food pictures

scissors

glue

paper fish

paper clips

paper fish pond

magnet on a string

Science Notebook

1 Cut out pictures of food. Glue each picture to a paper fish.

2 Put a paper clip on each fish. Put your fish in a paper pond.

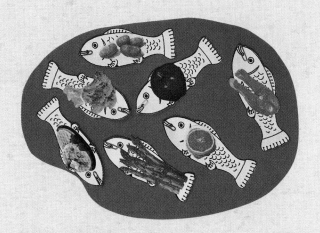

3 Use the magnet to fish for a balanced meal.

4 **Record** your meal by gluing your fish onto your plate.

Think! What makes a meal balanced?

Internet Field Trip

Visit **www.eduplace.com** to learn more about your favorite foods.

Combining Foods

Many people eat three meals a day. They eat breakfast early in the day. They eat lunch in the middle of the day. They eat dinner late in the day.

A **balanced meal** has food from many food groups. It has few fats or sweets.

The pictures show balanced meals. The first meal has food from three food groups.

The cereal is from one group. The milk in the pitcher is from another group. The fruit and juice are from a third group.

Reading Check Draw a picture of a balanced meal. Which food group is each food from?

Which foods make healthful snacks?

Activity
Testing Snack Foods

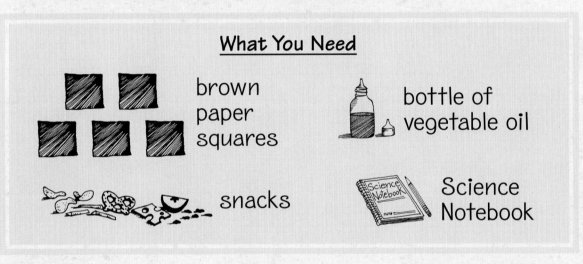

What You Need

brown paper squares

bottle of vegetable oil

snacks

Science Notebook

1 Write **oil** on one paper square.
Put a drop of oil on that square.

2 Write the name of each food on a different paper square. Rub each square with the food it names.

3 Hold each square up to the light. **Compare** each square to the square with oil. **Record** what you see.

Think! Which snacks are more healthful than others? Tell why you think so.

Good Snacks

Food you eat between meals is a **snack**. Some snacks are good for your body. Some are not.

There are snacks that have a lot of fat and oil in them. Potato chips and doughnuts have fat and oil in them.

The picture shows many foods. These foods
make healthful snacks. Fruits are good snacks.
Vegetables are good snacks. Snacks can be
from more than one food group, too.

Pretend you are making a healthful snack.
What would you put on the plate?

The pictures show good snacks from different parts of the world.

▲ This Russian bread can be filled with meat, fish, eggs, or vegetables.

▲ People in Lebanon serve these yogurt and vegetable dips with pita bread.

KEEPING FIT AND HEALTHY

▲ People in Mexico eat nachos as a snack.

 Make a card like the one below. It shows what you need to make 2 servings of nachos. Double the amounts to show what you need for 4 servings.

NACHOS		
Food	2 Servings	4 Servings
Tomatoes	1	2
Green Onions	1	
Shredded Cheese	5 tablespoons	
Tortilla Chips	6	

Reading Check **Draw a picture** to show healthful snacks you and your friends enjoy.

Word Power

If you need help, turn to the pages shown in blue.

Match the words with a picture. (E4–E7, E10–E11)

balanced meal   food group   food pyramid

1.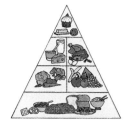

2.

3.

Use these words to fill in the blanks.

serving   snack   balanced

4. Food you eat between meals is a _____. (E14–E15)

5. An apple is one _____ of fruit. (E4–E5)

6. A meal with food from different food groups is a _____ meal. (E10–E11)

Solving Science Problems

Look at the list of foods. What would you choose for a balanced meal? Tell why.

milk	grapes	cheese sandwich
fish sticks	cookie	carrot sticks
popcorn	yogurt	ham sandwich
peanuts	peach	noodles and cheese

People Using Science

Dietitian

A dietitian talks with people about the kinds of food they need and how much food they need to stay healthy.

Dietitians work in places like hospitals and schools to plan healthful meals.

Where else might a dietitian be useful?

Using Math — Using a Bar Graph

A class made a graph of their favorite fruits.

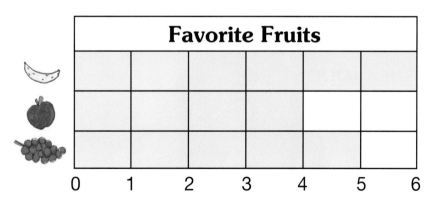

Use the graph to answer the questions.

1. How many children like best?

2. How many children like 🍌 and in all?

3. How many more children like 🍌 than 🍎?

How does exercise help your body?

Activity
Exercising Our Muscles

What You Need

6 exercise cards

Science Notebook

1 Choose an exercise card. Show the card to your group.

2 Do the exercise with your group.

❸ **Talk about** which muscle you used the most. **Record** your ideas.

Exercising Muscles	
Exercise	**Which muscles we use the most**
crunches	
knee bends	

❹ **Repeat steps 1–3,** using the other exercise cards.

Think! How do your muscles feel after you exercise them?

Find Out More!

Ask your classmates questions about their favorite ways to exercise. Make a tally chart to record your data. Then put the data into a bar graph.

Moving Muscles

You have bones in your body. You have muscles in your body. **Muscles** help you move.

As you move, you **exercise** your muscles. Exercise makes muscles and bones stronger. Exercise helps your body stay healthy.

Look at the pictures. The children are playing. They are moving in different ways. The boy is jumping rope. He is using the muscles in his arms and legs. What are the other children doing? What muscles are they using?

> **Reading Check** **Write a story** about friends exercising to stay healthy.

How do muscles and bones work together?

Activity

Measuring Muscles

What You Need

 2 construction paper strips

 scissors

 glue

 Science Notebook

1 Using Math

Put your arms at your sides. Have your partners **measure** around your upper arm with a paper strip. Mark the length.

2 Take the paper strip off your arm. Cut the strip at the mark. Glue the strip on a chart.

3 Make a muscle. Have your partners **measure** your arm again with another paper strip. Mark the length.

4 Cut the paper strip at the mark. Glue the strip on the chart. **Compare** the strips. **Record** your findings.

Think! How did the size of your arm muscle change? Why did this happen?

Muscles and Bones

Look at the pictures. The children are making funny faces. They are moving their muscles to make faces.

Muscles and bones work together. Muscles pull on bones to make the bones move.

Muscles in your face can help show how you feel. Make a face that shows you are happy. Feel the muscles and bones that make your face move. Do the same thing for a sad face. Compare how your muscles moved each time.

Reading Check Use your muscles and bones together. **Act out** your favorite animal.

Why do you need sleep?

Activity

Recording My Sleep

What You Need

Science
Notebook

1 Find out how many hours you slept last night.

2 Color one box on a graph for every hour you slept.

Using Math

3 Repeat steps 1 and 2 for each night.

4 **Record** how you felt before going to sleep and after waking up.

Think! How much sleep do you need? Tell why you think so.

Find Out More!

Look at your graph. Predict how much sleep other children your age need. Plan a way to show how many hours most children sleep. Tell about what you find.

Rest and Sleep

Look at the pictures. Follow the boy through his busy day. First, the boy walks to school. He is getting exercise.

Next, the boy does work at school. Then he plays outside. After that, he rests a little.

You **rest** by sitting or lying down quietly. What things does the boy do after he rests?

Look at the last picture. The boy is sleeping. Your body rests when you **sleep** at night. You need rest and sleep to stay healthy.

> **Reading Check Tell** about ways you rest each day. Why are rest and sleep important?

LESSON 7

What are good health habits?

Activity

Observing Clean and Dirty Hands

<u>What You Need</u>

2 wet wipes

paper towel

soap and water

Science Notebook

1 **Predict** whether your hands are clean or dirty. **Record** your prediction.

2 Wipe your hands with a wet wipe. **Record** what you find out.

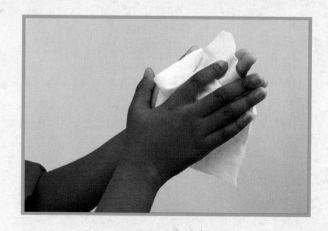

3 Wash your hands with soap and water. Then rinse and dry your hands.

4 Wipe your hands again with another wet wipe. **Record** what you find out.

Think! Why is washing your hands with soap and water important?

Good Health Habits

Germs can make you sick. They are very small.
You can't see germs. But they are all around.

Good health habits help you stay well. You
can wash with soap to kill germs. You can use a
tissue to keep germs from spreading.

Look at the picture. Find people who are showing good health habits. Can you find the boy who is using a tissue when he sneezes?

Now find people who are not showing good health habits. What are they doing?

✔ **Reading Check** **Write** a list of good health habits. Share the list with a classmate.

How can you keep teeth healthy?

Activity

Brushing Out Stains

What You Need

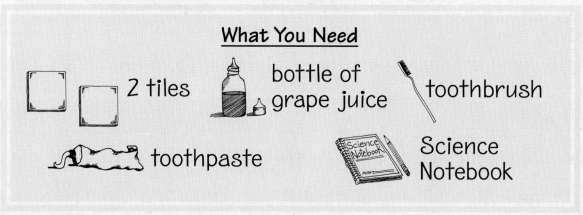

☐ ☐ 2 tiles   bottle of grape juice   toothbrush

toothpaste   Science Notebook

1 Put 2 or 3 drops of grape juice on two tiles. Let the tiles dry.

2 Use a toothbrush to brush tile 1. **Record** what happens.

3 Put toothpaste on the brush. Brush tile 2. **Record** what happens.

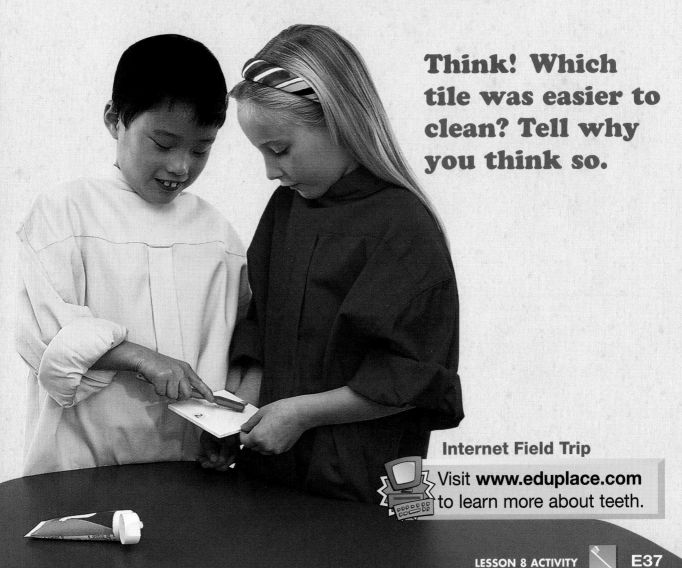

Think! Which tile was easier to clean? Tell why you think so.

Internet Field Trip

Visit **www.eduplace.com** to learn more about teeth.

Caring for Teeth

Cleaning your teeth keeps them strong and healthy. Eating balanced meals also helps keep your teeth strong and healthy.

Look at the picture. The girl wants strong and healthy teeth. What things will help her?

She can eat an apple. It is a healthful food.
She can **brush** her teeth with a toothbrush
and toothpaste. She can use thin string called
floss to clean between her teeth.

What things are not good for her teeth?
Candy and other sweets are not good for teeth.

A trip to the dentist's office can help keep your teeth healthy. A dental hygienist might take pictures that show what is inside your teeth. Then he or she will clean your teeth.

The dentist looks at the pictures. Then the dentist fixes any teeth that need it.

◀ **dental hygienist**

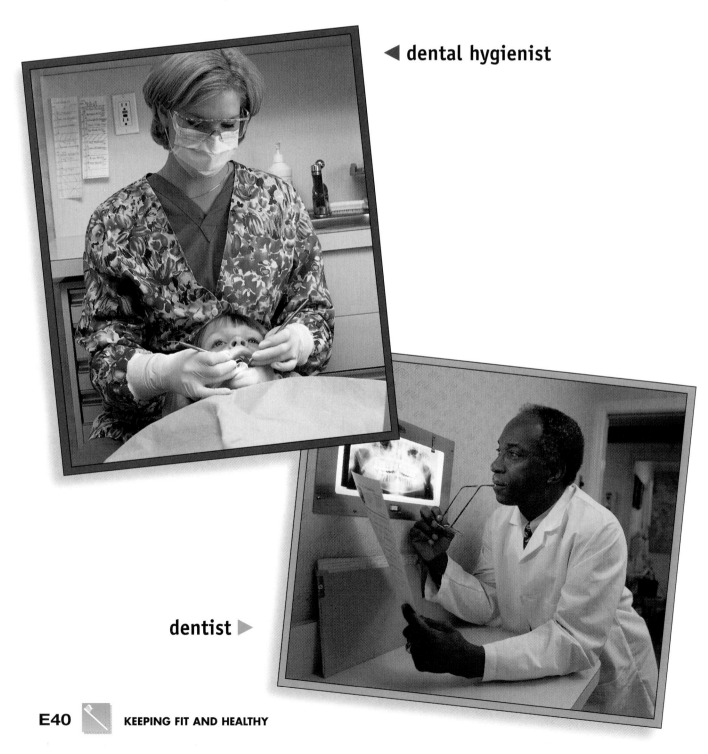

dentist ▶

KEEPING FIT AND HEALTHY

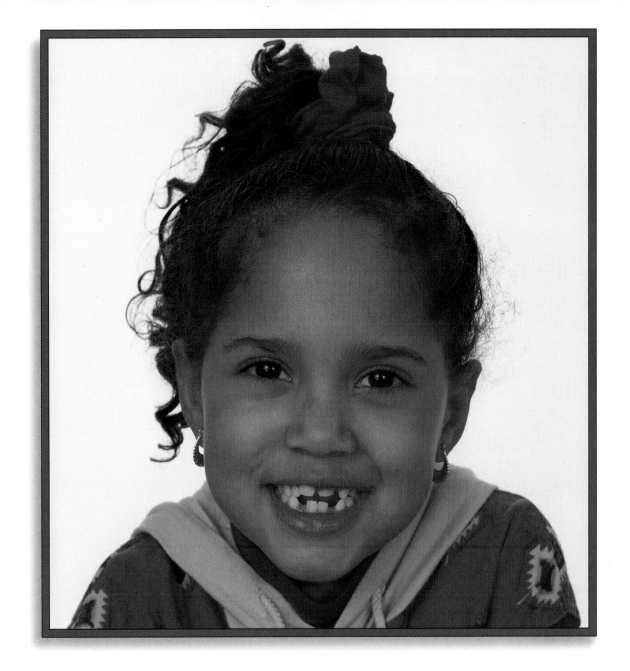

Have you lost any teeth? Many children start losing their baby teeth when they are about six years old. You need to keep your mouth clean even when you lose some teeth. That gives your new teeth a healthy place to grow.

Reading Check Tell a story about a tooth. How does its owner keep it healthy?

Word Power

If you need help, turn to the pages shown in blue.

Match a word with a picture. (E22, E31, E39)

sleep   exercise   brush

1.    **2.**    **3.**

Write the letter of the correct word.

4. You use a thin string called _____ to clean between your teeth. (E38–E39)

    a. floss   **b.** rest   **c.** brush   **d.** food

5. Your _____ help you move your body. (E22–E23)

    a. rest   **b.** sleep   **c.** muscles   **d.** germs

6. You _____ by sitting or lying down quietly. (E30–E31)

    a. brush   **b.** rest   **c.** muscles   **d.** exercise

7. Good _____ help you stay well. (E34–E35)

    a. floss   **b.** brush   **c.** serving   **d.** health habits

8. The _____ tells how many servings of food your body needs. (E4–E5)

    a. dentist   **b.** rest   **c.** healthful   **d.** food pyramid

Using Science Ideas

How is running helping to keep these men fit and healthy?

Writing in Science

Look at the picture. Is this a healthful meal? How could you make it more healthful? List the foods in your more healthful meal.

Main Idea

Read the story below. Then choose the sentence that tells the main idea.

> Good health habits help your body stay well. Exercise makes your muscles and bones stronger. Washing your hands helps keep germs from spreading. Brushing and flossing help keep your teeth strong. Rest and sleep help your body, too.

a. Exercise makes your muscles and bones stronger.

b. Good health habits help your body stay well.

c. Rest and sleep help your body, too.

d. Washing your hands helps keep germs from spreading.

Using Math · Using a Schedule

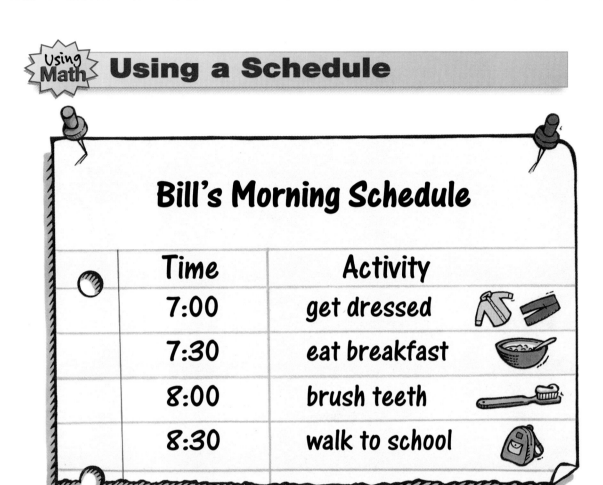

Bill's Morning Schedule

Time	Activity	
7:00	get dressed	
7:30	eat breakfast	
8:00	brush teeth	
8:30	walk to school	

Use the schedule to answer the questions.

1. What does Bill do at 8:30?

2. At what time does Bill get dressed?

3. Does Bill brush his teeth before or after he eats breakfast?

4. At what time does Bill eat breakfast?

SCIENCE and MATH TOOLBOX

Using a
Hand Lens

A hand lens is a tool that makes objects look bigger. It helps you see the small parts of an object.

Look at a Coin

1. Place a coin on your desk.

2. Hold the hand lens above the coin. Look through the lens. Slowly move the lens away from the coin. What do you see?

3. Keep moving the lens away until the coin looks blurry.

4. Then slowly move the lens closer. Stop when the coin does not look blurry.

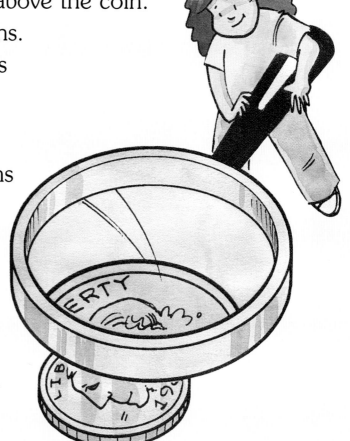

Using a
Thermometer

A thermometer is a tool used to measure temperature. Temperature tells how hot or cold something is. It is measured in degrees.

Find the Temperature of Water

1. Put water into a cup.

2. Put a thermometer into the cup.

3. Watch the colored liquid in the thermometer. What do you see?

4. Look how high the colored liquid is. What number is closest? That is the temperature of the water.

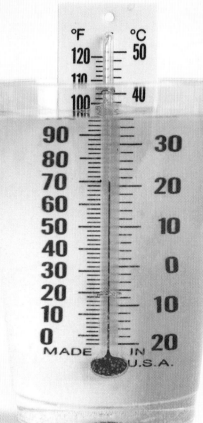

Using a
Ruler

A ruler is a tool used to measure the length of objects. Some rulers measure length in inches. Other rulers measure length in centimeters.

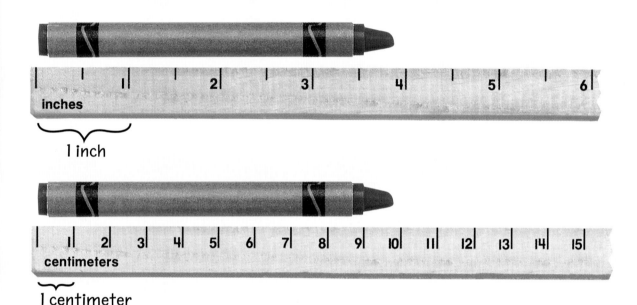

Measure a Crayon

1. Place the ruler on your desk.

2. Lay your crayon next to the ruler. Line up one end with the 0 mark on the ruler.

3. Look at the other end of the crayon. Which number is closest to that end?

Using a
Calculator

A calculator is a tool that can help you add numbers. It can also help you subtract numbers.

Subtract Numbers

1. Tim and Anna both grew plants. Tim grew 8 plants. Anna grew 17 plants.

2. How many more plants did Anna grow? Use your calculator to find out.

3. Enter [1] [7] on the calculator. Then press the [−] key. Enter [8] and press [=].

4. What is your answer?

Using a
Balance

A balance is a tool used to measure mass. Mass is the amount of matter in an object.

Measure the Mass of Clay

1. Check that the pointer is on the middle mark of the balance. If needed, move the slider on the back to the left or right.

2. Place a clay ball in one pan.

3. Add masses to the other pan until the pointer is at the middle mark again.

4. Add the numbers on the masses to find the mass in grams of the clay.

5. Add more clay to the ball. Repeat steps 3 and 4. How did the mass change?

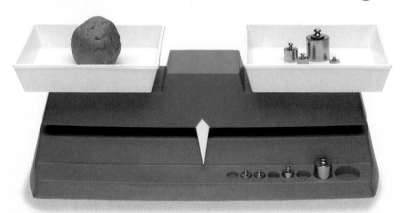

Making a Chart

A chart can help you sort information, or data. When you sort data it is easier to read and compare.

Make a Chart to Compare Animals

1. Give the chart a title.

2. Name the groups that tell about the data you collect.

3. Carefully fill in the data in each column.

How Animals Move	
Animal	**How it moves**
fish	swim
dog	walk, swim
duck	walk, swim, fly

Which animal can move in the most ways?

Making a
Tally Chart

A tally chart helps you keep track of items as you count.

Make a Tally Chart of Kinds of Pets

Jan's class drew pictures of their pets. You can make a tally chart to record the number of each kind of pet.

1. Every time you count one pet, you make one tally.

2. When you get to five, your fifth tally should be a line across the other four.

3. Count the tallies to find each total.

Kinds of Pets		
Pet	**Tally**	**Total**
Bird	III	3
Dog	ⵊⵊ I	6
Fish	I	1

How many of each kind of pet do the children have?

Making a Bar Graph

A bar graph can help you sort and compare data.

Make a Bar Graph of Favorite Leaves

You can use the data in the tally chart to make a bar graph.

Favorite Leaves

Leaf	Tally	Total
Oak	IIII	4
Ash	⁄HT I	6
Maple	II	2
Birch	III	3

1. Choose a title for your graph.

2. Write numbers along the side.

3. Write leaf names along the bottom.

4. Start at the bottom of each column. Fill in one box for each tally.

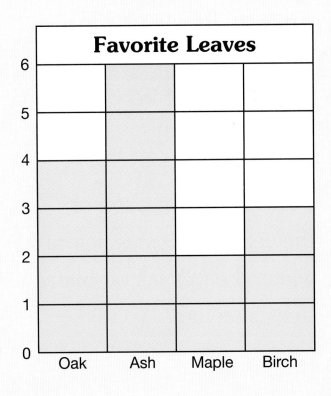

Favorite Leaves

Which leaf is the favorite?

GLOSSARY

A

animals Living things. They can move from place to place. Animals have body coverings. They eat other animals or plants for food. (A16)

attract To pull toward itself. A magnet attracts things made of iron, steel, and nickel. (C4)

autumn The season of the year that comes before winter. Leaves fall off many trees in autumn. (B33)

B

balanced meal Includes foods from most of the food groups on the food pyramid. (E10)

bar magnet A long, straight piece of steel that has been magnetized. A bar magnet attracts things made of iron, steel, and nickel. (C14)

bird A two-legged animal with feathers and wings. A bird is the only animal that has feathers covering its body. (A42)

boulder A very large rock. (D38)

breeze A gentle wind. The breeze makes a flag wave slowly. (B19)

brush To clean one's teeth. When you brush your teeth, you remove food bits from them. (E39)

calm When the air is calm, no wind is blowing. (B19)

clay soil Soil that has a lot of clay in it. Clay soil sometimes is found below topsoil. (D5)

cloud A group of tiny drops of water in the air. Rain falls from some clouds. (B26)

compass A tool that is used to show direction. The needle of a compass always points north. (C39)

compost Made by recycling once-living things. It can be added to soil to help plants grow. (D42)

cone The part of some nonflowering plants where seeds grow. Seeds grow between the scales of a cone. (A12)

exercise Moving your body. Playing outdoors is good exercise. (E22)

feathers Body covering of birds. Feathers keep birds warm. (A23)

fish An animal that lives in water. It has gills for breathing and fins for swimming. Many fish have scales. (A42)

floss Thin string used to clean between teeth. Flossing removes food a toothbrush cannot reach. (E39)

flower A part of some plants. Seeds form in a flower. (A8)

fog A group of tiny drops of water in the air. Fog is a cloud close to the ground. (B26)

food group A group of like kinds of food. Apples and bananas are part of the same food group. (E6)

food pyramid Shows the different food groups. The food pyramid also shows how many servings of each group you should eat each day. (E4)

good health habits Habits that help you stay well. Washing your hands before you eat is a good health habit. (E34)

hair Body covering of mammals. Hair helps mammals stay warm and protects their skin. (A22)

heat One kind of energy. The heat from the sun warms the earth. (B14)

hibernate To sleep through the winter. Some squirrels hibernate. (B43)

ice Water that is in the form of a solid. Ice is hard and cold. (B24)

lake A body of water with land all around it. Water flows into lakes from rivers. (D22)

leaves Parts of plants. Leaves make food for the plants. Leaves grow on stems or up from the roots. (A9)

life cycle The order of changes that occur during the lifetime of living things. Plants and animals have life cycles. (A46)

like poles Two south poles or two north poles of different magnets. Like poles repel each other. (C23)

living thing Something that is alive. Living things need air, water, and food to grow. (D9)

magnet A piece of metal that attracts things made of iron, steel, and nickel. (C4)

magnetic field The area around a magnet. It is where the force of the magnet works. (C28)

magnetic force A force that attracts things made of steel, iron, or nickel to a magnet. Magnetic force can go through air. (C8)

mammal One kind of animal. Mammals are covered with hair. They feed milk to their babies. (A40)

meat eater An animal that eats other animals. Meat eaters have sharp teeth to tear their food into pieces. (A35)

migrate To move from place to place as the seasons change. Some birds migrate south for the winter. (B42)

muscles Body parts that help you move. The muscles in your legs help you run and jump. (E22)

needles
Thin and pointed leaves. The shape of needles helps keep water in the plant. (A13)

nonliving thing
Something that was never alive. A rock is a nonliving thing. (D9)

ocean
A great body of salt water. An ocean is larger than a lake. (D19)

once-living thing
Something that was alive at one time or was once part of a living thing. A feather and an acorn are once-living things. (D8)

plants
Living things that need water, light, and air to grow. Most plants have roots, stems, and leaves. Many have flowers. (A8)

plant eater
An animal that eats plants. A plant eater has flat teeth for grinding food. (A35)

poles The places on a magnet where the magnetic force is strongest. On a bar magnet, the poles are at the ends of the magnet. (C17)

recycling Using something again. Compost is made by recycling once-living things. (D42)

repel To push away or force apart. Like poles of two magnets repel each other. (C23)

rest To lie down or sit quietly. After you exercise, you should rest. (E31)

ring magnet A round, flat piece of metal that has been magnetized. It has a hole in the middle. The poles of a ring magnet are on the two flat sides. (C15)

river A body of water. It flows in a long path. Rivers flow downhill into lakes and oceans. (D18)

root A plant part. Roots grow down into the soil. Roots take in water from the soil. (A9)

sand Very small rocks. Some ocean beaches are covered with sand. (D39)

scales Body covering of some fish and reptiles. Scales are thin and flat. (A23)

scratch To make a mark on something. A harder rock will scratch a softer rock. (D32)

season A time of the year. Spring, summer, autumn, and winter are the four seasons. (B32)

serving The right amount of a food that you should eat. A serving of cereal may be 1 cup. (E5)

shade An area that is out of the sun. It is often cooler in the shade. (B11)

shelter A safe place to live. A nest is shelter for a bird. (A29)

skin A covering for the bodies of animals. Skin can be protected by hair, feathers, or scales. (A22)

sleep A period of rest. When you sleep, your body refreshes itself. (E31)

snack Food you eat between meals. Fruits are healthful snacks. Potato chips and candy are unhealthful snacks. (E14)

spring A season of the year. It comes after winter. In spring many plants begin to grow. (B33)

stem A plant part. Water and food move through stems. Some stems are hard. (A9)

stream A narrow path of flowing water. Streams are smaller than rivers. (D19)

strong wind A wind that blows fast and hard. A strong wind will blow paper down the street. (B19)

summer The season that comes after spring. Summer is the warmest season. Days are longer in the summer. (B33)

sunlight The light of the sun. Sunlight warms the earth. (B11)

T

temperature The measure of heat in an object. Temperature is measured by using a thermometer. (B5)

temporary magnet A magnet that works only for a short time. A temporary magnet can be made by stroking a metal object with a magnet. (C34)

topsoil A top layer of dark, loose soil. Most plants grow well in topsoil. Worms live in topsoil. (D5)

unlike poles The south pole and the north pole of different magnets. Unlike poles attract each other. (C22)

water vapor Water that is in the form of a gas. You cannot see water vapor. (B24)

weather The temperature, wind, precipitation, and other conditions in the air. Weather changes from day to day. (B4)

wind Fast-moving or slow-moving air. Wind can make objects move. (B18)

winter The season that comes after autumn. It is the coldest of the four seasons. Days are short in the winter. (B33)

INDEX

CREDITS

ILLUSTRATORS
Cover Liisa Chauncy Guida.
Think Like a Scientist 2–7: Benton Mahan. 10–11: Laurie Hamilton. *border* Liisa Chauncy Guida.

Unit A 1: Bob Pepper. 4–5: Dave Schweitzer. 12–13: Anne Feiza. 16–17: Bob Pepper. 18–19: Sharon Hawkins Vargo. 28–31: Patrick Gnan. 34–35: Randy Hamblin. 36–37: Phil Wilson. 46–47: Robert Roper. 48: Sharon Hawkins Vargo. 51: Liisa Chauncy Guida.

Unit B B: Sharon Hawkins Vargo. 1: Nancy Tobin. 4–5: Nancy Tobin. 6: Andrew Shiff. 10–11: John Jones. 20–21: Denise and Fernando. 28: Sharon Hawkins Vargo. 32–33: Ellen Appleby. 48: Sharon Hawkins Vargo. 50: Jim Durk. 51: Saul Rosenbaum.

Unit C C: Jerry Pavey. 1: *t.* Jerry Pavey, *b.* Sharon Hawkins Vargo. 18: *t.* Sharon Hawkins Vargo, *b.* Dorothy Stott. 22–23: *background* Julie Carpenter, *wooden toys* Jerry Pavey. 40, 43: Sharon Hawkins Vargo.

Unit D 4–5, 14–15: Robert Roper. 22–23: Rose Mary Berlin. 24–25: Sharon Hawkins Vargo. 45: Nathan Young Jarvis. 46: Sharon Hawkins Vargo. 48: Julie Durrell.

Unit E 4–7: Dan Brawer. 17–19: Sharon Hawkins Vargo. 30–31: Barbara Gray. 34–35: Jenny Campbell. 38–39: Ruth Flanigan. 42–43: Sharon Hawkins Vargo. 44: Susan Drawbaugh. 45: Ruth Flanigan.

Science and Math Toolbox *logos* Nancy Tobin. 5: Randy Verougstraete. 7–8: Randy Chewning. 10: Randy Verougstraete. *border* Liisa Chauncy Guida.

Glossary 10–18: Sharon Hawkins Vargo. 19: Tom Pansini. 20: Sharon Hawkins Vargo.

PHOTOGRAPHS
All photographs by Houghton Mifflin Company (HMCo.) unless otherwise noted.

Cover *t.* Mark Tomalty/Masterfile Corporation; *m.r.* Craig Tuttle/The Stock Market; *b.l.* Peter Gridley/FPG International; *b.r.* Tim Davis/Tony Stone Images.

Unit A A: Michael Fogden/DRK Photo. 8–9: George Hunter/Tony Stone Images. 9: *t.* Walter Chandoha; *m.* Darrell Gulin/DRK Photo; *b.* Hans Pfletschinger/Peter Arnold, Inc. 12: *l.* Arthur R. Hill/Visuals Unlimited; *r.* Fritz Polking/Peter Arnold, Inc. 13: Ron Watts/Corbis; *r.* Richard Kolar/Animals Animals/Earth Scenes. 19: D. Demello/Wildlife Conservation Society, Bronx Zoo. 22: *t.l.* © Stephen Collins/Photo Researchers, Inc.; *t.r.* © Thomas Martin/Photo Researchers, Inc.; *b.l.* Darryll Schiff/Tony Stone Images; *b.r.* Zefa Germany/The Stock Market. 23: *t.l.* John M. Roberts/The Stock Market; *t.r.* Thomas Kitchin/Tom Stack & Associates; *b.l.* Thomas Kitchin/Tom Stack & Associates; *b.r.* Brian Parker/Tom Stack & Associates. 24: *t.l.* Stephen J. Krasemann/Tony Stone Images; *t.r.* © Bill Dyer/Photo Researchers, Inc.; *b.l.* Miriam Austerman/Animals Animals/Earth Scenes; *b.r.* Zig Leszczynski/Animals Animals/Earth Scenes. 25: *b.l.* © Tim Davis/Photo Researchers, Inc.; *b.r.* Brian Parker/Tom Stack & Associates. 34: Art Wolfe/Tony Stone Images. 35: S. Purdy Mathews/Tony Stone Images. 36: C. Allen Morgan/Peter Arnold, Inc. 36–37: Stephen Dalton/Animals Animals/Earth Scenes. 37: Michael Fogden/DRK Photo. 40: *t.l.* Sue Streeter/Tony Stone Images; *t.r.* Charles Krebs/Tony Stone Images; *b.l.* Mike Bacon/Tom Stack & Associates; *b.r.* © Gregory Dimijian/Photo Researchers, Inc. 41: *t.l.* Jeanne Drake/Tony Stone Images; *t.r.* © Jim Steinberg/Photo Researchers, Inc.; *b.l.* © Nick Bergkessel/Photo Researchers, Inc.; *b.r.* Fritz Prenzel/Tony Stone Images. 42: *t.l.* Lynn M. Stone/DRK Photo; *r.* E.R. Degginger/Color-Pic, Inc.; *b.l.* © Charles V. Angelo/Photo Researchers, Inc. 43: *l.* Norbert Wu/Tony Stone Images; *r.* Zefa Germany/The Stock Market. 46: *t.l.* Alan G. Nelson/Animals Animals/Earth Scenes; *t.r.* Wayne Lankinen/DRK Photo; *b.* Stephen J. Krasemann/DRK Photo. 47: *t.l.* Tom Lazar/Animals Animals/Earth Scenes; *t.r.* Wayne Lankinen/DRK Photo; *b.* Stephen J. Krasemann/DRK Photo. 50: *t.l.* John Warden/Tony Stone Images; *t.m.* © Treat Davidson/Photo Researchers, Inc.; *t.r.* Stephen J. Krasemann/DRK Photo; *b.l.* © Suzanne L. Collins/Photo Researchers, Inc.; *b.m.* © Jany Sauvanet/Photo Researchers, Inc.; *b.r.* David Northcott/DRK Photo.

Unit B 4–5: *r.* Grant Huntington for HMCo. 14–15: Don & Pat Valenti/DRK Photo. 18–19: Oldrich Karasek/Tony Stone Images. 19: *t.* Tony Freeman/PhotoEdit; *m.* Chris Hackett/The Image Bank; *b.* Wes Thompson/The Stock Market. 20: *m.* © E.R. Degginger/Photo Researchers, Inc.; *b.* © Renee Purse/Photo Researchers, Inc. 21: John P. Kelly/The Image Bank. 24–25: Richard Hutchings for HMCo. 25: Richard Hutchings for HMCo. 26: W. Hille/Leo de Wys. 27: *l.* D. Cavagnaro/DRK Photo; *r.* Superstock. 29: Dwayne Newton/PhotoEdit. 36: Tony Freeman/PhotoEdit. 37: Bob Skjold/PhotoEdit. 40: Hans Reinhard/Bruce Coleman Incorporated. 41: Wayne Lankinen/Bruce Coleman Incorporated. 42: Walter Edwards/National Geographic Society Image Collection. 42.43: S. Nielsen/Imagery. 43: Richard Biegun/FPG International. 46–47: Eric A. Soder/Tom Stack & Associates. 49: Richard Hutchings/PhotoEdit.

Unit C 8–9: Ken Karp for HMCo. 19: *t.* David R. Frazier Photography. 39: *t.* Grant Huntington for HMCo.

Unit D 1: Stephen J. Krasemann/DRK Photo. 18: Tim Davis/Tony Stone Images. 18–19: Wayne Lankinen/DRK Photo. 19: Stephen J. Krasemann/DRK Photo. 24: E.R. Degginger/Color-Pic, Inc. 25: Anne Kuhn/Dwight R. Kuhn. 32: Murrae Haynes for HMCo. 33: *t.r.* © Charles D. Winters/Timeframe Photography Inc./Photo Researchers, Inc.; *b.r* A.J. Copley/Visuals Unlimited. 34: *t.l.* E.R. Degginger/Color-Pic, Inc.; *m.r.* E.R. Degginger/Color-Pic, Inc.; *b.l.* E.R. Degginger/Color-Pic, Inc. 35: *r.* Steven Frisch/Stock Boston. 38–39: Superstock. 39: Parvinder S. Sethi. 42–43: Bill Field/Field Photography. 44: *b.l.* Aaron Hahpt/Stock Boston; *b.r.* David Lawrence/The Stock Market.

Unit E E: *r.* Steven Mark Needham/Envision. 10: Steven Mark Needham/Envision. 10–11: Rick Ostentoski/Envision. 11: Steven Mark Needham/Envision. 16: *t.* Vladimir Morozov/Envision; *b.* Amy Reichman/Envision. 22–23: *inset* Bob Daemmrich Photography. 23: Tim Davis/David Madison Photography. 43: © Catherine Ursillo/Photo Researchers, Inc.